Thailand

Live – Love - Retire

A.L. Harlow

1

www.Al-Harlow.com

Introduction

I moved to Thailand the first time in 2002, and I stayed for nearly 10 years. I've recently moved back again. I've learned some things along the way and I wish to share them with you in this book.

First and foremost, you should read this book because you want to start and succeed in a new life in what can be paradise.

Secondly, you should read this book so that your dream of paradise does not become a living hell.

Moving to Thailand to live out your golden years is for many people a huge step. It means leaving both family and familiarity in your home country. For some these losses become burdens that draw them back to the warmth and comfort of their home country.

Unless you have unlimited funds it means changing many of your dietary habits. Thai food in Thailand is nothing like Thai food in your home country.

Living in Thailand can be inexpensive and rewarding if you are willing to integrate and learn some new ways of living and this book will show you how.

This book will give you a good head start to make a smooth transition as an expat in Thailand and it will help you to avoid the often stupid mistakes that have seen many expats flounder and go home or worse, find they are living off of and on the streets.

If you want to move to Thailand and live a wonderful life, you will have to do things the right way. Respect the people, their culture, and their laws.

Table of Contents

Before You Leave Home

Before you leave home there are a few things you need to take care of.

PASSPORT: Make sure you have at least 18 months left before your passport expires and that you have plenty of blank pages. If you have less than 2 years left, I would actually advise you to get a new one because depending on where you live in Thailand you may have to travel a long distance to have it renewed when the time comes. For instance, I live in the north of Thailand and recently had to renew my passport. To renew my passport I had to travel to Bangkok for a process that took only 10 minutes. This 10 minute task meant I had the expense of airfares, taxis, hotel room for 1 night and meals. This cost me a sum that was a little north of 10,000 baht on top of the 6000 baht for my new passport.

VISA: Though there are many different visas one can get the most common one sought by retirees is called a Non-O visa. This will be discussed in more detail later in the book but before you come to Thailand you should contact your closest Thai Embassy and apply for a 90 day Non-O visa. A 90 day Non-O visa can be converted to what many people call a retirement visa but is actually a 1 year extension of stay. You can only apply for and get a 90 day Non-O visa in your home country.

HEALTH AND VACCINES: Be sure to purchase a decent travel insurance policy to cover you for at least your first 90 days. Insurance for longer terms will be explained later in this book.

It would be a good idea though not mandatory to make sure your vaccinations are up to date to see what vaccinations you need visit this site http://www.tmb.ie/destinations/vaccinations-for-thailand

LIFESTYLE: Think about the life style you want to enjoy. Do you want to live near a beach? Do you want to live in a big city? Do you want to live in a rural area? Do you want to live somewhere that has the amenities of a big city without the traffic hassles? Do you want to live where it is hot and humid year round? Do you want to live where it is slightly cooler and there is respite from the heat for about 4 months every year?

IMPORTANT PAPERS: If you have a degree, bring the original and the transcripts with you. I will explain why later in the book. If you are divorced, bring an original copy of your divorce decree. Again, I will explain why later in the book.

Deciding Where To Live

CHIANG MAI: Is known as the Rose of the North and is situated about 600 kilometers north of Bangkok. It has a large expat community and the climate is, in my opinion pleasant. The summer is hot but not as hot as Bangkok and the humidity, though stifling, is more tolerable than further south. The winter is very pleasant. The city's surroundings are beautiful. There's also less pollution except during the burning season. The burning season begins in February and continues until March. This burning occurs throughout Northern Thailand, Burma, Laos and Cambodia. The city is picturesque and you can enjoy a nice lifestyle there. There are many restaurants and bars that cater to the many expats that call Chiang Mai Home. Rental costs in Chiang Mai tend to be a bit higher than other northern cities but food is cheaper. Chiang Mai also has the added benefit of an international airport catering to many routes. To learn more about Chiang Mai, visit this site.:

http://www.visitchiangmai.com.au/

CHIANG RAI: Chiang Rai is 180 kilometers north of Chiang Mai and is 60 Kilometers from the fabled Golden Triangle. The weather is even cooler than Chiang Rai and with less the half the population, there is even less traffic, noise and pollution noise and pollution with the exception of burning Season. From February through March of every year the locals burn rice straw. This happens in all of Northern Thailand, Burma, Laos, Cambodia and Southern China. Again, during burning season many people choose to go south for a month holiday. The entertainment is mainly focused around a small area called Jed Yod road and there are not many restaurants that serve western dishes and those that do are more expensive than they were at home. Chiang Rai also has an international airport but except for a few flights to China, the planes all fly to and from Bangkok. This can be a deterrent to people who like to travel a lot because the only option is to fly to Bangkok then catch a flight to wherever you want to go. House rentals in Chiang Rai are quite inexpensive ranging from as low as 5000 baht for a basic 2 or 3 bedroom houses to 30,000 baht per month for a relative mansion. To learn more about Chiang Rai visit this site:

http://www.thailand-guide.com/chiangrai/

PHUKET: Pronounced POOKET, is home to a very large expat community. Phuket's main attraction is the beach though I believe the beaches near Krabi are superior. Service in Phuket is second rate and in general, Phuket very expensive. I can recommend it for a holiday but not for living. If you do wish to live there rent something far from the beach and you will find they are quite cheap. To learn more about Phuket visit this site:

https://www.phuket101.net/10-quick-facts-about-phuket/

KHON KAEN: If you travel about 2 hours North of Korat you come to Khon Kaen. Khon Kaen is a regional city and is home to two large Universities. Many of the expats that live here previously lost all their money when they lived in Pattaya. Unless you are married or have to be there for employment I would avoid Khon Kaen. To learn more about Khon Kaen visit this site

http://www.khonkaenlink.info/eng/.

HUA HIN: Hua Hin is the oldest beach city in Thailand. Most of the expats living in Hua Hin are Scandinavians with little knowledge of both the Thai culture and the Thai language. Unless you are working there, Hua Hin will soon wear you out. Hua Hin also has a reputation of being the most violent and expensive city in Thailand! To learn more about Hua Hin visit this site:

http://www.tourismthailand.org/AboutThailand/Destination/Hua-Hin.

PATTAYA: Pattaya, situated by the sea is big on adult entertainment it is home to a world famous night Walking Street. There are about 80 go-go bars and an uncountable number of beer bars. There are three major shopping centers in Pattaya and an abundance of good restaurants. For rentals a good choice would be one of the Thai style condos in the area of Naklua and Jomtien. Pattaya is not for the people who are not open minded about different lifestyles. To learn more about Pattaya visit this site:

http://www.pattayaconcierge.com/.

BANGKOK: Bangkok is Thailand's biggest city and its capital. Many people say it is the best choice for expats. It has many job opportunities and there thousands of good restaurants catering to all the world's major cuisines.

Bangkok's public transportation is excellent with a SkyTrain and the Metro servicing all major parts of this huge. Bangkok is, in the minds of many, kippers nickers. To learn more about Bangkok visit this site:

https://bangkokattractions.com/fun-facts-about-bangkok/.

MY TWO TOP CHOICES FOR RETIREMENT ARE: Chiang Mai and Chiang Rai. If you want to work however, there is no choice better than Bangkok.

Getting Your Retirement Extension

All of the forms you need, if you do the visa application yourself, can be downloaded by visiting this site:

http://donslifeinthailand.com/Immigration_Forms.html

First and foremost, to qualify for a retirement extension (visa) you must be 50 or over.

Okay, hopefully you arrived in Thailand with a 90 day Non-O visa. If you did not enter on a 90 day Non-O visa, don't bother reading this section. The next step is to get that visa changed to a 12 month retirement extension. You do not need to jump on this right away, but you do need to make the application 45 days before the expiration of your 90 day visa. You will also need to open a bank account and deposit at least 800,000 Baht or show proof of income of 65,000 Baht per month. The easiest bank to open an account is Bangkok Bank other banks all seem to require a work permit to open an account. Why you ask? I don't know.

There are two ways to do this extension, you can do it yourself for 1900 Baht or you can pay an agent 5000 Baht or more to do it for you. Either way you do have to go to the immigration office to sign the papers. Everything you need to know to get the visa is on this site:

http://www.thaiembassy.com/retire/retire.php

If using 800,000 Baht in a Thai bank you will need a letter from your bank manager showing your balance and that the funds have been on deposit for at least 2 months, the letter should be no older than 7 days and no joint or restricted accounts will be accepted.

This is tough to do since you have not been in the country for 2 months yet so I recommend that if possible you do your first extension based on monthly income. To prove monthly income you can go make a statutory declaration at your embassy stating your income.

IMPORTANT: Every photocopy or form you present must be signed by you. If you are presenting a TM.18, whoever filled it out must sign the copy also.

Rental Options

There is not much one can say about rental options except that it is possible to rent a house, a condo, a serviced or non-serviced apartment. The prices will be dictated depending on where you choose to live. In Chiang Rai or Chiang Mai as mentioned before, you can rent a house for anywhere from 5000 Baht per month to 25,000-30,000 baht per month. Condos rent for slightly more, 8,000 baht up; serviced or non-serviced apartments are similarly priced to condos.

Obviously, the further from the city center you choose to live, the cheaper the rents will be. If you can, avoid the real estate agents catering to westerners because they inflate the prices a LOT.

If it is possible, you will save money if you have a Thai GF or wife who can negotiate a rental for you. After a deal has been struck she can take you back and show it to you then you can decide to take it or not.

Just be aware that Thais will always charge westerners more so don't show your face too early. Even if you find a Thai friend you can trust (and they are rare) to do the leg work for you for a daily fee of say 500 – 600 Baht it would be better than going to an estate agent.

Visit this site to find rental properties in Thailand:

https://www.thailand-property.com/properties-for-rent

Should I Learn The Language

Many people in English speaking western countries complain about immigrants who could not speak English. Yet Westerners come to Thailand and expect to be understood, and make no effort to learn to speak Thai.

Some of the reasons I hear are "It's too hard", "I'm too busy" and "why should I, my friends speak English". I am not fluent in Thai but I do make an effort to learn a few new words or phrases every day.

If you plan on spending the rest of your life in Thailand, if you plan on having a Thai girlfriend or wife and if you want to be accepted by the Thais it is important to learn at least the basics of the language.

Based on my experience, I'll give you the reasons I think it is important that you learn to speak. It is also a good idea, if you can, to learn to read Thai.

1. You will have a better understanding of the Thai people & their culture.

2. You will be able to understand the way Thai people communicate.

3. You will get an understanding of the basic aspects of the Thai culture

I could write a long list but I think you understand what I am saying. As you learn more you will begin to get a better understanding of the Thai people and find it easier to integrate into the community, you will be able to make Thai friends and shop at the Tha Lard (market).

My Thai is far from perfect, but I can convey what I want and avoid misunderstandings. I think that if you decide to have a Thai girlfriend you should both to try and learn each other's language and culture. For your Thai partner to learn English and you not learn Thai hardly seems fair.

Be smart and learn the Thai Alphabet. There are many online sites where you can learn that.

Can Thais and westerners become friends? Sure they can. I have a Thai friend I met two days after my arrival who spoke little English but we got along like a house on fire and now 6 years later he's picked up more English, I've picked up more Thai and we are great friends.

Anyway making an attempt to learn the Thai language is always appreciated by Thai people and they get a lot of enjoyment from helping you learn more.

The the West, especially Europe, is on a downward trend whilst South East Asia is growing. Because of this there are an ever growing number of westerners that are moving to Thailand. Many are seeking, or will seek, employment and if they can speak Thai they will have a lot of leverage in any profession.

Working In Thailand

As a retiree on a retirement extension you are not permitted to work in any capacity including volunteering or assisting your wife, if you have one, in her business. If you are married and are on a marriage visa it is possible to get a work permit.

Many retirees work as English teachers in private schools but to work in a government school you must be under 60 years of age. Most teaching jobs will require that you possess and can produce a degree and transcripts to be eligible for work, though a few private schools are willing to waive this requirement.

Visit: http://www.thethailandlife.com/jobs-thailand-expats to see some of the opportunities for working in Thailand.

Visit: http://www.thaiworkpermit.com/prohibited-occupations-in-thailand.html to see a list of jobs you cannot do.

WORKING ONLINE: Many people work online. If you do, do it at from home not in an internet cafe. If the work you do is conducted outside of Thailand such as English coaching to Japanese or Chinese students the chances of getting in trouble are slim at best. But if you think about teaching English on Skype to someone in Thailand don't! Anybody can inform immigration about what you are doing if they have a bone to pick with you. Not only could a Thai person inform immigration, it is not unheard of for other expats to do it too. Learn more about working online here http://www.chiangmailocator.com/wiki-can-digital-nomads-legally-work-in-thailand-how-p131

Cost Of Living

Let's face it, one of the main reasons people move to Thailand is because it is much cheaper enabling them to live better on their pension than in their own country. But while housing is very cheap, if you always want to eat western food, that can get pretty expensive. If you enjoy imported foods such as cheese, wine, olives you can still have it but not as often. Designer clothes and branded beauty products are not cheap either.

Having said that, Thailand still ranks as one of the cheapest places to retire. In general I find it cheaper than Cambodia, The Philippines, Laos and Malaysia.

Here is a great site to compare the cost of living with the city you now live in:

https://www.numbeo.com/cost-of-living/in/Bangkok

Please keep in mind that if you're thinking of living in another city like Chiang Mai, Chiang Rai or Khon Kaen, the cost of housing will be cheaper; however, food items and entertainment will be about the same.

If you plan on living in Koh Samui or Phuket, then you won't save much, if any depending on your drinking habits. In general, you may spend less for rent on the islands, but will probably be more expensive and you will in all likelihood spend more on socializing.

Chiang Mai and Chiang Rai are about 25% cheaper than Bangkok.

A Final Note on Living Costs

If while you're reading this you begin thinking, "wow, I thought Thailand was a lot cheaper than that", don't let these numbers dissuade you.

If you don't mind living in a smaller studio apartment and traveling a little bit further to get into the city and are able to eat street food, you can get by on 20-25, 000 Baht per a month.

You can buy bulk fruit in the big market rather than buying daily from food stalls, and you can choose to ride the Baht bus instead of taxis. There are always many ways to save money, and the reality is that many Thai people live quite well on a salary of 15-20,000 Baht or less per month.

So work out what's important to you; what are your "must-haves" and "can do with-outs".

If you're retired with a pension and a savings account, then keeping a close watch on your pennies may not be necessary. But it always makes sense to manage your budget.

Also additional expenses arise from time to time and you'll need to budget for these. Some of these expenses may be travel, life and health insurance, vehicle insurance and registration, fuel costs and replacing items that break like a computer or phone. Just make sure your budget takes into account emergencies.

Thai Women:
Where To And Where Not To Find Them

Thai women are reputed for their beauty, fiery temper and family loyalties and are everywhere you look.

If you want to find a girlfriend remember a few pointers

They don't go to beer bars or work in massage parlors and rent themselves out for the night.

You won't find them hanging out on chat rooms.

They rarely show the skin on their shoulders.

She will be nervous about you meeting her family; a bad girl won't because you are probably one of many.

A bad girl, will never pay nor even offer to pay, a good Thai girl likes to share.

A good Thai girl will always be accompanied by a friend on your first few dates.

A good Thai girl will not sleep with you on the first or even the second date. In fact a good Thai girl will not sleep with you until she is confident that you are a good person and that you are committed to a long relationship.

A good Thai girl, dresses conservatively, speaks politely and doesn't use bad language.

These are just a few traits of god Thai ladies. But I hope you get the message that it's not smart to start a relationship with bar or massage girls. You are looking for trouble. If you can hire them for a night so can someone else.

Use acquaintances to meet a good Thai lady. If you do meet one, don't count on her speaking English; so believe me, unless you make a sincere effort to learn Thai, things can and will be misunderstood.

It is easy to find failed Thai–western relationships; in fact they are the majority. But most of these failed because the man was thinking with the little head rather than the big head. Face it, if a fat old western man thinks the bar or massage girl 30 or 40 years his junior is in love with him and not his money he is a fool. When he buys her a house and business and she leaves him with nothing he has only himself to blame.

After you've been with your partner for a while and you're just not sure they are sincere, tell her your money is all gone. If she stays and wants to help you, take good care of her, you found a winner. If she leaves, though you may be heart broken, you probably just saved yourself a lot of money and grief.

Buying A House

The only way to buy a house in Thailand, unless it is a condo is to put it in the name of a Thai person you can trust such as a girlfriend, wife, business or lawyer. Having said that, finding someone you can trust 100% is not an easy task. Foreigners are not allowed to own land in Thailand. If you are interested in buying you have two options:

You could get a 30-year leasehold on the land or purchasing it through a limited company.

You can purchase an apartment or condo.

Legal restrictions: Due to the legal restrictions in Thailand, many foreigners seek other ways to buy property.

It is possible for a foreigner to lease land for 30 years. So in many cases a foreign man, if he is married, can purchase land in his Thai wife's name. In cases like this, the Thai wife forms a lease contact with her husband.

Another way to purchase land is by setting up a Thai Limited Company. However, to do this 51% of the company must be owned by a Thai citizen. With just a little bit of brain power, it is easy to imagine the many dangers and risks in doing this. But hey, the worst that can happen is you either lose your money or have a fatal accident.

Due to these legal restrictions most foreigners simply buy a condo or apartment. However, as mentioned elsewhere in this book, don't consider this purchase as an investment in the future.

Cultural: Issues You Should Be Aware Of

Before we begin, here is an interesting article for you to read.

http://bangkok.coconuts.co/2016/07/29/five-stages-culture-shock-foreigners-thailand.

Many things in Thai culture are very different from your culture. For instance, you probably shake hands whereas Thais wai. You probably enjoy heated discussions; Thais will avoid confrontation in any form.

Here are a few dos' and don'ts in Thailand.

Most Thais will think you are a tourist. Understanding this basic point of view will give you a head start on understanding the ways to deal with people you meet.

First you must understand that Thais fit other people into of three groups.

The first and most important group is close relatives. These are family members.

The second group is neighbors, customers and business partners. Thais will always act politely and friendly towards this group because they may pose a danger.

Lastly is the stranger, that's you. Thais do not trust this group so they will try to manipulate them.

This categorization of groups is simplified but it contains a lot of truth.

You might think someone overcharged you and you may consider the person to be bad. That conclusion would be very wrong; the person was just good at making an income. Were you cheated on the purchase? No, to the seller, whatever you bought was worth whatever they can get you to pay; so if you paid too much it was your fault.

When you want to get someone's attention such as flagging a taxi, keep your hand horizontal with your fingers down. If your fingers are up, in Thai culture, it is considered rude.

Never clap, snap your fingers, or whistle to get attention unless you are summoning a dog.

Always dress respectfully when you visit a temple. White is a safe color. Women should not wear mini dresses or short shorts and they should keep their shoulders covered.

Speak quietly in temples. If monks are worshiping either keep it to a whisper or preferably be silent!

Always remove your shoes and hat when entering a temple.

Never sit with your feet pointing towards the Buddha. You may sit cross-legged as in a meditation position or on the back of your calves so your feet are facing behind you.

In Thailand and many other Asian cultures the feet are considered to be the lowest and least clean part of the body. Many things we westerners do with our feet such as pointing at something or holding a door open are considered poor taste so don't do it. Also, unless you have been given permission never touch another person's head and never, ever, should you touch a monk.

Thailand's Royal family is held in very high esteem by Thai people. There are pictures of His Majesty and the royal family everywhere. Never speak or act disrespectfully towards any member of the Royal family. If you drop a coin, don't even use your foot to stop it because it bears an image of royalty. Thailand has very strict Lese Majeste laws, and breaking one can and often does attract a 15 year stay in a Thai prison.

Questions, visit:

http://www.asiaobserver.org/on-thailand-lese-majeste-law.

Thais are very fussy about personal hygiene. Showering at least daily is essential!

For the most part Thais do not know your culture or customs so don't expect them to follow your cultural idiosyncrasies'.

Thais do not like to say "no" so instead they will say "Yes, but..." For instance, if you ask for a Pepsi and they do not have Pepsi they may say "Yes, but will Coke be okay." Do not take as a sign of silliness it is just their way of being polite.

Thais often lie about little things. For example if you ask for directions to some place, they will answer you even if they don't know the answer. To them this is not lying, they do so they do not lose face.

The Royal Thai Police if called to the site of any incident will generally expect a foreigner to pay them for their help. But you can be sure that the Thai person will always be believed before a foreigner is.

Driving In Thailand

Your home country driving license is only valid for 90 days. After that you will need to secure a Thai license. This is a relatively simple process of getting a doctor's note to say you are fit to drive, filling out a form taking an eye and coordination test then having your photo taken and parting with about 250 Baht. Initially you will be issued a 1 year license and when you renew you will get 5 years.

Driving in Thailand is fraught with danger. For the inexperienced it is downright scary. Driving a car is best because you do have a certain level of protection. Driving a motor bike is something I would never do though many expats belong to motor bike clubs. Generally however they do not ride their bikes in the city. Most of their activities take place on quiet country roads.

In Thailand we drive on the left side of the road and the rules are based on the British traffic laws. Notice I say based on because they are not always, or maybe I should say, they are rarely followed. When I first arrived I thought that I would be relatively safe if I followed the rules regardless of how others drive. Boy was I wrong; you have to learn to drive like a Thai if you expect to survive long on the roads. I have since evolved into a creature with eyes not only in the front but also the back and sides of my head. I was involved in two expensive accidents by driving like I was taught and I do not intend to be in another one. These accidents were expensive primarily because I am a foreigner and we are wrong in any circumstance by default unless you can prove the other party wrong. Remember Thais will believe Thais before they believe a foreigner. Now I do not drive without two things. First is my wife, to present my case if I have an accident and as further proof I have front and rear video cameras. Am I paranoid? Yes I am but with good reason.

A car flashing its headlights at you is not conveying a polite message. It doesn't mean "I'm letting you go first", it means do not get in my way because I will not slow down for you.

Some foreigners are also very dangerous. Some are not used to driving on the left hand side of the road and some don't have a clue about how Thais drive. If you rent a motorbike in Thailand, especially in touristy areas, beware of the foreigners because often they are more dangerous than the locals.

Don't expect to see warning signs on the road like you do at home. Oftentimes when driving you may come upon a poorly or un-marked work area. Also it is common to come upon roads with dangerous curves where dozens of people die every year that have no warning signs. Basically, if you want to survive, don't drive too fast if you don't know the road and always be on the lookout for the unexpected.

Roundabouts are uncommon in Thailand and Thais do not know how to use them. When entering a roundabout Thais expect vehicles already in the roundabout to give them right of way. My best advice is when in roundabouts, drive very slowly.

Usually it is allowed to turn left even if the traffic light is red. However, this is not the case at all intersections. Look for a sign that indicates "free left turn", and observe the traffic light: if there is an arrow light on the signal, wait until it turns green.

You are probably accustomed to the left lane on highways being the slow lane. The reality in Thailand is that it is considered just another overtaking lane. Be aware at all times if you want to move left.

Drugs In Thailand

Thailand's Drug Laws are very strict and the penalties are very harsh.

There is no minor penalty if you get caught with even as little as one gram of marijuana, and the police do not use any discretion on small amounts of class B drugs.

Still, year in year out, embassy staff get called to visit Thailand's infamously hard prisons to talk with foreigners caught using or possessing drugs.

The visit always ends with the same words: "You're in a lot of trouble".

If you get caught with an amount the police consider is enough to charge you as a dealer you can only pray for a pardon from the King sometime in the next 50 years.

Just stay away from Drugs

It's easy to get carried away in a group when a joint gets passed round. But if you get caught with that joint you could find yourself locked up in an unpleasant cell with real criminals.

If people are smoking a joint weed and offer you a puff, whether they are Thai or foreigners just say no and depart. If the police come they will arrest everyone not just those in possession.

The Drug Classification Law in Thailand can be viewed here. http://www.thailandlaw.org/drug-laws-in-thailand.html

Anyone caught breaking these laws will be punished by imprisonment or death.

Be aware that you may be randomly subjected to stop and search. Both foreigners and Thais can and are stopped and searched in the streets of Thailand.

You should also be aware of how the law relates to prescription drugs containing illegal drugs.

Information for travelers with prescription medications containing narcotics, or psychotropics in or out of Thailand.

http://www.thaiembassy.org/bucharest/contents/files/travel-20120907-191945-489473.pdf

If You Decide To Get Married

If you decide to get married there are a few things you need to consider not the least of which is that you are often not only marrying the girl, you are marrying the whole family who will expect you to be generous. Often there will be a payment to the parents called sin sot (dowry) the amount is negotiated and dependent on what you are prepared to pay. Often if the girl has been married before or the parents are deceased there is no dowry.

Many Thai women have children from a previous scoundrel that they married thinking mistakenly, that he was in it for the long term. Not only is he no longer in the picture, he also in all likelihood does not help to support his children.

If you spend enough time around Thais you will soon learn about Thai family values. Having said that, I know a few westerners who have lived here for many years and still don't fully understand the scope of a Thai's connection with their family. It is vitally important to understand these family values if you're married to a Thai.

Most Thais live with their families while they are attending university and most of these continue to live with their family after they graduate. When Thais get married, most will continue to live with either his or her parents even when they have children. The general thinking is, why separate their parents from their grandchildren? And probably more importantly, why spend your money on another house if you can help your parents and live cheaper? This is actually a good thing when mum and dad retire; unless they worked for the government the pension is only about 700 Baht per month and the parents need the help. You could consider it to be the Thai social security system.

To Thais, family values means, if a Thai has to make a decision and the choice means going against the parent's wishes or against the wishes of their spouse, they will go against the spouse every time. The same decision process is applied for all members of the family. Any outsider, including you will come second. Since their parents did everything for them growing up, as adults, it is their turn to reciprocate and support their parents.From my observations, it seems that most often it is the daughters who contribute most to supporting their parents. So, if you marry a Thai lady and expect her to give up her job (if she has one) be prepared and willing to assist in the support of her parents. If you can't accept this, don't marry!

Thais would never consider putting their elderly parents in an aged-care home.

In many Thai families everyone sleeps in the same room. Married adult children when visiting will most often sleep in the same room as the rest of the family including parents, brothers, sisters, and their spouse.

Thais are much closer to their families than western families and are in general quite happy about it. Overall, these strong family bonds make Thais much happier people and for that, I envy them.

Finally, there are two ways to get married in Thailand. The first is a legal marriage with a marriage certificate issued by the local Amphur. For this marriage you will have a little leg work to do. For a detailed, step by step process click here

Getting married in this way will see your marriage being legally recognized in your home country.

The other way to get married is a traditional Thai wedding which essentially is a simple ceremony that can be done in your home followed by a reception. The reception can be as large or small as you choose. Many couples simply invite their friends to a hotel for the buffet lunch which of course you will pay for. This marriage has no legal standing and will not qualify you for a marriage visa or a work permit. It also will not bind you to sharing your assets should the marriage fail. Most people I know that have this kind of wedding do so because they are not yet divorced from their wife back home.

The Good The Bad and The Ugly

I really like living in Thailand. I respect and like the culture and the people, the weather suits me fine, and the language is not too hard to learn if you have a good teacher. Is Thailand perfect, no but it is the right place for me. There are negatives but I have learned to ignore them and just get on with living. However, I would be doing you a disservice if I did not make you aware of the negatives.

So these are some of the not so positive issues about Thailand.

Visas – It is not really a visa, it is a 12 month extension of my 90 day Non-O visa and I have to renew it every 12 months.

Weather - The weather is great for about 4 months a year.That means that 8 months a year can be not so great. In the north November, December, January, and February are usually wonderful. February through March is the burning season and sometimes the smoke is so bad I wear a mask outside or just stay indoors. The remainder of the year is either hot or hot and rainy.

Double pricing – Some, but not all Thais believe that foreigners have more money.So they pay higher prices for entry to places like museums and national parks. Sometimes the admission to a particular attraction for a Thai may be 200 Baht and for a westerner 400 baht or more. This policy has filtered all the way down to Tuk-Tuk drivers and street venders. There is no way to avoid it, if a Thai sees a westerner the price will, unless it is marked, always be higher.

Real Estate –As mentioned before, you cannot own land here but you can, and many do, buy a condo. Others get around the land buying restrictions by putting it in the name of a Thai (friend, wife, girlfriend, lawyer), which is often a really bad idea. Another big mistake is thinking of real estate as an investment to profit on in the future. Thai real estate does not follow the same trends as in their home country. Thais look at a house that has already been lived in similar to a used car. Thais would rather buy a new house or car. Personally, I recommend renting and keeping your money.

Culture - Thai culture and your culture are very different in many facets and ways. Making a cultural mistake in Thailand is as easy as pointing at something with your foot. We are lucky though because most of the time Thais will usually just laugh at our ignorance.

Language - The amount of English spoken in Thailand is very low. Of the 10 ASEAN countries, Thailand falls in 8th place. Globally it is about the 74th position. Even though Thais study English beginning in the first grade and through high school and college, most cannot speak a complete English sentence. In school they are taught grammar, reading and writing but not conversation.

Health: Thailand has some health problems that you should be aware of. Some of the maladies Expats are faced with are Diarrhea, dysentery, dengue fever, bacterial infections, and parasites. Thankfully the hospitals and doctors that are quite good at diagnosing and treating most of the stuff you can catch here.

Safety: The single largest threat to your safety is when you are driving. Also you must be careful as a pedestrian. Not many Thais will stop to let you cross the road even though you may be at a pedestrian crossing. Pedestrians do not have the right of way here.

Motorcycles can be very dangerous but the danger can be reduced if you wear a decent helmet that costs more than the typical 200 baht a Thai will spend. If you must ride a motorcycle, drive very slowly and be aware and alert to everything around you at all times. To be relatively safe on the roads, always look in every direction twice, always give right of way to the other guy, never drink and drive, but assume that everyone else is. Don't automatically drive off because the traffic light is green; look in both directions first because someone else may be running the red light. I think Thais consider and amber light as a signal to accelerate and a red light as a suggestion to stop. Speed limits are also seen as suggestions.

Your assets - Just like everywhere in the world, there are plenty of scam artists wanting to take your money. The scam artist may be a younger woman who says she is "in love" with you, it may be a trusted business partner, it could even be your smiling landlord. Two of the most notorious groups are the Tuk-Tuk drivers and the guys renting out Jet Skis.

Protect yourself at all times and do not be gullible.

Health Insurance

Health insurance is something most expats struggle with. Though it can be cheaper than your home country, when you are, like most expats, living on a pension it can seem quite expensive.

If you are over 60 it gets hard to find an insurer that will accept you unless you are renewing and once you pass 70 nobody will take you at all, many not even for renewal.

The price of a policy for a 65 year old can range from 30,000 Baht per year to over 150,000 Baht per year depending on the coverage you want. If you want coverage in Thailand only it will generally be around 30,000 – 50,000 baht per year, if you want international coverage, (and I can't see why you would because if you go on holiday you can buy short term travel insurance) be prepared to pay a lot more.

Another consideration is that these policies will not cover pre-existing conditions. So, if you are like me and have diabetes, there is an 80% chance that when you are hospitalized for any of a number of reasons except an accident, it will be related to diabetes and all the money you spent on the policy will have been down the drain. Thus, I chose to save my money and put it in the bank for the day I need it. Basically I self-insure.

Most insurance policies will not cover treatment for cancer unless you pay extra, if in fact at all. Many of the less expensive policies also will not provide enough coverage for something like heart surgery or stroke.

For a good overview of this subject visit https://www.thailandstarterkit.com/health/thailand-health-insurance/.

Your Ongoing Success

If you decide to make Thailand your retirement home I wish you much success and have a few pointers before I finish this book.

Leave any pre-conceived notions at home and accept Thailand for what it is.

Don't have unrealistic expectations.

Don't expect things to be done the same way as they are in your country and don't complain when they aren't.

Respect the cultural values of your adopted country and remember you are a guest.

Remember also that you are in a sense an ambassador of your country so don't act like an idiot, act courteously and responsibly. Otherwise the Thai people just might assume everyone from your country is just like you.

Forget about schedules and plans. If you expect Thais to value promptness as you do, you will be disappointed often.

Take you shoes off before entering a home and many businesses. With businesses, if you are not sure simply look and if you see shoes outside the door, leave yours there too.

Don't express anger in public or with your wife if you marry.

Don't use foul language in public or with your wife if you marry.

If you find yourself complaining about everything and everybody, go home. You are not happy.

If you find yourself thinking about going home, remind yourself why you left. If that does not help, go home.

Acceptance and tolerance is critical if you want to maintain your sanity. You need to accept that some stuff here is different and tolerate what you do not agree with. There is very little you can do to change it anyway so why stress over it. Some people find it really simple others just find it too bloody hard.

Thailand will not make you happy. If you are not a naturally happy person nothing will change in Thailand. Initially you may feel relaxed and free but what and who you are will rise to the top soon. You know the old saying "You can take the boy out of the country but you cannot take the country out of the boy"

A Preview Of:

Common Sense Life Hacks

A Survival Guide to Achieving Your Goals And Improving Your Business And Personal Relationships

A.L. Harlow

Introduction

Everybody wants to succeed in life. Success is everybody's dream. Unfortunately though, it is not presented on a silver platter. The pursuit of success is the driving factor of most people's lives. Humans simply want better in their lives.

This book contains two hundred tips to help you to better your life and improve personal and business relationships. If you follow these tips you will be empowered and equipped to attain whatever realistic goals you set.

Here's some simple advice that has been given to many people; "If you do as you've always done you will get as you've always gotten."

The Grand Idea

Maintain The Proper Mindset

The right attitude must be maintained whether you are building a business or driving to work. Maintaining a good attitude is and always will be the number one precondition for achieving your goals. And frankly, it is the sole qualification that you will need.

Be Interested And Listen

Knowledge is power and if you are not listening, you will lack knowledge. Without knowledge you quite simply will have no direction. You don't have to know everything but it matters a lot to know what does matter.

Maintain Your Good Health

Do not be silly enough to think that you can make it on by intelligence alone. Consume proper amounts of food and water. If you neglect your health you can never accomplish your goal.

Use Your Common Sense

Here's a truth that smarts to hear or read about. Data has

piled up on the amount of people who lose everything they have because they didn't use common sense. It is pre-programmed into everybody and using it actually makes life in general much easier.

Smile a Lot

It's true! Smiling goes above almost all differences. Just think how much it would benefit your cause. It is not the most trivial of signals. Smiling is something that works to your benefit. This has been proven time after time.

About the Author

A.L.HARLOW was born in 1963 and grew up on the streets of Norwalk California. After spending much of my younger years battling drug addiction, he finally broke free in 2002. He has been married since 2008 and has one son. He holds a Diploma and several Certifications in Psychology and continues to learn every day. He is an artist, graphic artist, tattoo artist, writer and an addiction coach.

Al is also co-founder of the Adapt4Life Foundation. Adapt4Life is a non-profit organization working with homeless military veterans and civilians to get them off the street by teaching them the skills they need to succeed.

For more books visit: www.Al-Harlow.com